SELF-REFLECTION
30 Days Naked

MICHAEL TEAGUES

Copyright © 2018 Michael Teauges

All rights reserved.

ISBN: 0692118853
ISBN-13: 978-0692118856

PURPOSE OF JOURNAL

The purpose of this journal is to take a closer look at a mirrored reflection of you. These next 30 days will allow you to strip yourself and understand why you say or do certain things. What triggers a reaction? What triggers an emotion? What causes you to fight? What causes you to stay? What causes you to let go? What drives your love? What drives your passion? You will be able to look within yourself and reflect on your past, present, and future and work to change for a better you. A stronger you. A wiser you.

For myself, fitness gave me a reason, a drive, and a purpose. It's the key to my success! It made me feel alive and valid in a world that once made me feel lost. The key to success is getting to know yourself, your fears, your doubts, your ambitions, your drive, and your dreams, and to find what fuels your desire to push, and know that you can master anything you put your mind to.

MICHAEL TEAGUES

My goal with this journal is to encourage those who have been lost in the fire yet made it through the flames. Whether from broken souls, broken hearts, or broken homes, I want you all to know that you can RIZE above any situation. Keep pushing forward. No one stops you but YOU.

CONTENTS

Day 1	The Past	Pg #1
Day 2	Change	Pg #4
Day 3	Fear	Pg #6
Day 4	Dream	Pg #8
Day 5	Goals	Pg #11
Day 6	Treasures	Pg #13
Day 7	Darkness	Pg #15
Day 8	Success	Pg #17
Day 9	Love	Pg #20
Day 10	Cautious	Pg #22

CONTENTS CONT'D

Day 11	Thankful	Pg #24
Day 12	Surrounding	Pg #26
Day 13	Faith	Pg #29
Day 14	Choice	Pg #31
Day 15	Stand	Pg #34
Day 16	Life	Pg #36
Day 17	Vision	Pg #38
Day 18	Defeat	Pg #40
Day 19	Roots	Pg #42
Day 20	Imperfections	Pg #45

CONTENTS CONT'D

Day 21	Tolerance	Pg #47
Day 22	Connections	Pg #49
Day 23	Pain	Pg #51
Day 24	Patience	Pg #53
Day 25	Silence	Pg #55
Day 26	Release	Pg #57
Day 27	Strength	Pg #60
Day 28	Passion	Pg #62
Day 29	Beauty	Pg #64
Day 30	Naked	Pg #66

SELF-REFLECTION 30 DAYS NAKED

Day 1

The Past

To be productive and present, you must release the past. You must release past hurt, past pain, even people who are dragging you to an atmosphere you wish to abandon. The mind is so powerful! It will believe we can live in two atmospheres because that's what we force it to believe. We tell ourselves we can't, which allows confusion to overcome the heart and can cloud our judgment when moving forward. Everyone has a past, the key to surviving the future, is not to allow the past to overpower the present.

_____
_____
_____
_____
_____

MICHAEL TEAGUES

SELF-REFLECTION 30 DAYS NAKED

Day 2

Change

Change can sometimes be not so comfortable, yet its needed to grow and learn. Many people work hard to stay the same because they fear failure more than success. That small possibility keeps us stagnate in our flight to rise. Believe in every moment and more in your purpose. Never be afraid to step outside of the box. Nothing great is built with limitations nor while staying in your comfort zone. You must have self-confidence and believe in yourself to know you can soar higher than your vision can see.

_____
_____
_____
_____
_____
_____

SELF-REFLECTION 30 DAYS NAKED

Day 3

Fear

Fear is the darkness, the shadow, the doubt that sits within us which is created by us. It's a self-inflicted emotion that hinders and denies us access to our true selves. Fear is an emotion that limits you if you do not face it head on and overcome it. Once we put death to the emotion of fear, there will be no bondage, no obstacle, and no test not conquered.

_____
_____
_____
_____
_____
_____
_____

SELF-REFLECTION 30 DAYS NAKED

Day 4

Dream

Dreams keep us alive. Dreams keep us wondering. They give us thoughts of endless possibilities. When we stop dreaming, we stop living. These sporadic thoughts and images provide us with reason to push through to keep going, understanding our purpose, and believe in the idea of possibilities even when they seem impossible. Nobody stops you but you, believe in yourself, and everything is possible.

_____
_____
_____
_____
_____
_____

SELF-REFLECTION 30 DAYS NAKED

Day 5

Goals

Goals require focus, self-sacrifice, self-discipline, and willpower. These are the keys to success! We must remain steadfast, and vigilant through the sacrifice to meet the goals at hand.

_____
_____
_____
_____
_____
_____
_____
_____
_____
_____
_____
_____

Day 6

Treasures

One of the greatest treasures in the world is to raise the bar within you. To keep elevating beyond expectancy. Being able to broaden your spectrum gives life to your being. Be true to yourself, and always remain humble. Never forget where you come from and always remember where you're going.

Day 7

Darkness

Darkness surrounds the only place that the sun does not shine on, which shadows and outlines the sun itself. But in the darkness, we sleep, we rejuvenate, and we grow. Darkness can sometimes take us to our lowest points as well as our highest points. So, understand in the darkest hours, you became the greatest you.

_____
_____
_____
_____
_____
_____
_____
_____
_____

Day 8

Success

Success is not determined by financial gain. Success is a mind-state; it's an accomplishment! It's a sense of determination. It's knowing exactly who you are and what you're capable of. It's knowing you hold the key to open any door you set your mind to, and that's achieved by mental prosperity.

MICHAEL TEAGUES

SELF-REFLECTION 30 DAYS NAKED

Day 9

Love

Love has the capability of causing so much damage, yet all the possibilities to bring so much happiness. Love has the power to destroy; it has the power to heal, it has the power to unite, it has the power to alter one's vision. Understand love is not built on the outside; it is not built on another person, and it's not built within any temple. True love is built from within and flows out with a geniune passion which will never die.

_____

_____

_____

_____

_____

_____

SELF-REFLECTION 30 DAYS NAKED

Day 10

Cautious

Be cautious of your intake. What you feed the mind, the soul and the body will determine your elevation toward your destiny. If you continue to feed your body toxic love, advice, or thoughts, you will remain stagnate in this journey of life. If you feed your body positivity, determination, and drive, you will soar higher than you ever believed your wings could fly.

SELF-REFLECTION 30 DAYS NAKED

Day 11

Thankful

Be thankful for your whetherpath.... good or bad. Be thankful for today because there was no accident in the road that was paved for you. Things will not always be easy. Things will not always be justified. Things will not always be fair. Things will not always go your way. Yet, you will always have the choice to stride toward a better day. Another chance to be a better you.

SELF-REFLECTION 30 DAYS NAKED

Day 12

Surrounding

Always surround yourself with individuals who sharpen you, your focus, your passions, your will, and your desire to be more. Do not surround yourself with individuals that taint your vision and blur your thoughts. You become a product of who you surround yourself with, so surround yourself with the best.

_____
_____
_____
_____
_____
_____
_____

SELF-REFLECTION 30 DAYS NAKED

Day 13

Faith

Faith without any movement is a dead action. You must believe in yourself more than any of the eyes that are set on you. Nothing in life is impossible when you believe and have faith. However, with neither, all movement will cease and at that moment, you will have become paralyzed due to doubt from yourself. Have faith and wake the movement. Trust the process, in spite of what you see.

_____
_____
_____
_____
_____
_____

Day 14

Choice

No matter the circumstance, problem, or obstacle. Know that you have the power of choice, the power to change, the power to alternate, the power to rise above, stand tall, and the power to be great for a greater purpose. The choice is yours.

_____
_____
_____
_____
_____
_____
_____
_____
_____
_____

SELF-REFLECTION 30 DAYS NAKED

Day 15

Stand

You shall never fall if you aren't leaning on any excuses. You must be your own strength. You must believe in yourself. You must know who you are. Excuses are made for the weak. Stand tall and continue to rise above and defeat.

SELF-REFLECTION 30 DAYS NAKED

Day 16

Life

The craziest thing about life is that it always gives you a second chance to get it right, and it's called tomorrow. But, sometimes the second chance is missed, and tomorrow's not given. So, for that reason alone, you should live every day as if it's your last. Love unconditionally and always laugh when you can.

_____
_____
_____
_____
_____
_____

SELF-REFLECTION 30 DAYS NAKED

Day 17

Vision

We may not always have the choice of what is dealt to us, but we have the choice on how we look at it, how we receive it and how we embrace it. This gives us a clear vision on how to handle it. Changing the lighting in the same situation gives you a different view on how to deal with the situation. Never allow your vision to become blinded when dealing with what may seem to be a repeated situation.

_____
_____
_____
_____
_____
_____

SELF-REFLECTION 30 DAYS NAKED

Day 18

Defeat

Defeat starts with the mind and failure is a state of mind. Only you control the action upon the approach. If you believe you're a failure, then you have failed. But the victory is believing you can achieve anything you put your mind to. That is the power of the ultimate defeat.

SELF-REFLECTION 30 DAYS NAKED

Day 19

Roots

When the roots are deep, there is no reason to fear the wind. Roots are the foundation of which one should never forget the obstacles it took to become strengthened. Although you may be hit with storms from time to time. A true Queen of a King knows not to waiver due to its deepened roots.

_____
_____
_____
_____
_____
_____
_____
_____
_____

SELF-REFLECTION 30 DAYS NAKED

Day 20

Imperfections

Your imperfections are part of what makes you beautiful. Your scars, your scratches, your bruises, your flaws, that's what makes you imperfectly perfect. Never hide your imperfections. Never be ashamed of them. They are you, and that's what makes you beautiful.

MICHAEL TEAGUES

Day 21

Tolerance

Certain things in life are made to break you or make you great. Certain things make you question yourself; others make you realize exactly who you are. Examine what you tolerate. It can be the key factor in your uprising or your hindrance. Understand the lesson being given.

_____
_____
_____
_____
_____

Day 22

Connections

Many dead-end people will connect to a power source. To be a power source, please understand that at times, you will need to cut off your power lines to preserve you. Be cautious of the things that you allow or who and what connects to your energy. Know that it's ok to stray away from any connection where the vibe doesn't feel right because that negative connection can be the very thing that drains you.

_____
_____
_____
_____

Day 23

Pain

Sometimes we smile when our hearts are really crying. Sometimes we pretend to be happy to hide our truth. No one wants to feel hurt. No one wants to feel as if their world is falling apart and every breath ache. No one wants to have tears streaming down their face and doubt in their heart, but this pain is necessary to understand that what doesn't kill us only makes us stronger. Pain teaches us lessons that we didn't think we needed to learn but now know. Some of the greatest changes come from the deepest pains that we thought we couldn't survive.

_____

_____

_____

Day 24

Patience

You must be able to humble yourself and realize that timing is everything. It is easier to say, "have patience," than it is to practice patience. You must have self-control of all emotions, whether good or bad and balance it so well that nothing can shift the crown that you wear as a King or Queen.

_____
_____
_____
_____
_____
_____
_____
_____

Day 25

Silence

It's essential that we take the time to seclude ourselves. We must shut off our phones and shut out the world and learn to sit in utter silence. Self-care is important and loving yourself is necessary. It's been said that if you quiet the mind, the soul will speak. To do that, we must learn to stop moving, stop talking and listen. Take the time to refuel yourself. Take the time to work on you and better yourself. Take the time to breathe in the silence that surrounds you.

_____
_____
_____
_____
_____
_____
_____
_____

Day 26

Release

Hoarders are those who do not like to get rid of anything because if they do, they feel as if it's throwing away a piece of them. As individuals, we can sometimes harbor feelings that we do not want to get rid of but need to release to grow mentally and spiritually. We must be able to release the past and anything that hinders our growth and trust the process of healing. So, release, relax and repeat as often as needed to ensure nothing is blocking your growth.

_____
_____
_____
_____
_____
_____
_____
_____

Day 27

Strength

Our strength doesn't come from what we accomplish, or what we can do. Our strength comes from battles we've endured, and from struggles we came face-to-face with, in moments we thought we were too weak to defeat. Our strength isn't dependent on another person! Our strength comes from within us. We hold the key to believing in ourselves. Nobody stops you but you. No matter how many times life knocks you down, or you feel like you can't push through, you owe it to yourself to be more! Keep going, and you will find your greatest strength.

_____
_____
_____
_____
_____
_____
_____

SELF-REFLECTION 30 DAYS NAKED

Day 28

Passion

Find out what drives you in life. What is it that you want to do in life? What brings you joy and inspires you to be more? What is your motivation? What is it that drives you every day? You must find your passion in life. Your passion will determine your purpose, your reason, your being. Your passion will allow you to do what you love and find endless happiness within it.

_____
_____
_____
_____
_____
_____
_____
_____
_____

SELF-REFLECTION 30 DAYS NAKED

Day 29

Beauty

Everything has beauty. It takes a believer to see and recognize it. Beauty is skin deep. Some people cannot see true beauty because they are only focused on the outer appearance. Your skin tone, your shape, your weight. That's not what makes one beautiful; that's just a bonus. It's your mind, your heart, your soul, and your confidence! There is not one person on this earth who should make you feel as if you're not beautiful enough. Recognize the beauty you have and own it.

SELF-REFLECTION 30 DAYS NAKED

Day 30

Naked

To be stripped away from self. To be stripped away from doubt and fear leaves you naked in the truth. Sometimes the truth is hard to accept because we allow our pride and ego to overpower our emotions at times. We sometimes run from the truth because we are scared to look in the mirror and accept the painful reality of who we are. We fear self-reflection which is key when understanding our actions. We don't realize the pain of the truth brings comfort in realizing who we are. The truth is needed. The truth is how you find you.

_____
_____
_____

ABOUT THE AUTHOR

Naked the Poet

My name is Michael Teagues. Best known as Myk Tea or Naked the Poet. I am a mentor as well as a personal fitness trainer.

I was born in Kansas City, Kansas. At the age of six, I was rescued by my Uncle Kevin from an abandoned project home with no windows, doors, or food. I laid wrapped in a blanket along with my siblings next to my cocaine-addicted alcoholic mother. My siblings and I resided with my uncle until he and I moved to the Fillmore District of San Francisco. As I became older, the struggle to avoid the negative influences of my peers, violence, and gangs on a day-to-day basis became almost impossible. My uncle wanted better for us, and when I was seventeen, he decided we move out of California for a fresh start in Las Vegas, NV. I attended Cheyenne High School and later transferred to Valley High School, where I later graduated. After high school, I pursued a career in writing. I wanted to show others in my own words, in my experience who had been through the same struggles and pain, that you do not have to become a product of your environment, a positive change is always possible.

As time passed, I became influenced by the array of political negativity regarding being a minority in what seems to be an unfair world, and this pushed me to seek change in myself. I began to seek answers to questions that flooded my mind regarding religion, *and numerous topics and issues, but what stood out the most was the prejudice of being a black man in our society. I had to open my mind and reset my mindset and give light to the shaded areas of my mind and heart. I had to re-evaluate life and its meaning to create a legacy, using the negatives I faced, the roadblocks and fears, to Rize above the concrete barrier of the world.*

To speak my truth, I became nude, raw, uncut, and unfiltered. I stripped myself and became NAKED.

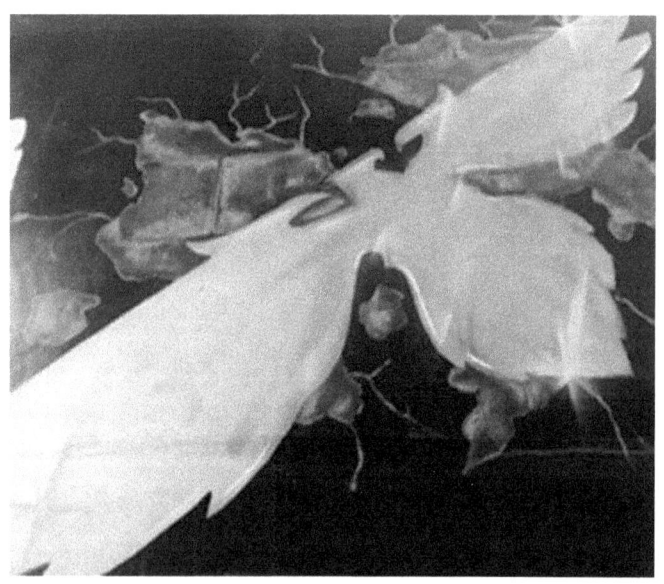

www.ingramcontent.com/pod-product-compliance
Lightning Source LLC
LaVergne TN
LVHW041634070426
835507LV00008B/627